Like a Yeti Catching Marmots

T0057270

Like a Yeti Catching Marmots

A LITTLE TREASURY OF TIBETAN PROVERBS

Pema Tsewang, Shastri

WITH JOSH BARTOK

WISDOM PUBLICATIONS • BOSTON

Wisdom Publications
199 Elm Street
Somerville MA 02144 USA
www.wisdompubs.org

© 2012 Pema Tsewang Shastri
All rights reserved.

No part of this book may be reproduced in any form or by any means, electronic or mechanical, including photography, recording, or by any information storage and retrieval system or technologies now known or later developed, without permission in writing from the publisher.

Library of Congress Cataloging-in-Publication Data
Padma-tshe-dban, Sastri.
Like a yeti catching marmots : a little treasury of Tibetan proverbs / Pema Tsewang Shastri.
p. cm.
Proverbs in Tibetan and English, with pref. and explanations in English.
ISBN 1-61429-000-8 (pbk. : alk. paper)
1. Proverbs, Tibetan—Translations into English. I. Title.
PN6519.T55P33 2011
398.9'9541—dc23

2011028941

ISBN 9781614290001
eBook ISBN 9781614290155

16 15 14 13 12
5 4 3 2 1

Cover design by Phil Pascuzzo. Interior design by Gopa&Ted2. Set in Cronos Pro 10.5/14.7.

Wisdom Publications' books are printed on acid-free paper and meet the guidelines for permanence and durability of the Production Guidelines for Book Longevity of the Council on Library Resources.

Printed in the United States of America.

MIX Paper FSC FSC® C011935

This book was produced with environmental mindfulness. We have elected to print this title on 30% PCW recycled paper. As a result, we have saved the following resources: 10 trees, 3 million BTUs of energy, 962 lbs. of greenhouse gases, 4,336 gallons of water, and 275 lbs. of solid waste. For more information, please visit our website, www.wisdompubs.org. This paper is also FSC® certified. For more information, please visit www.fscus.org.

This book is dedicated
to the long life of the
Tibetan culture.

Preface

It's said that nothing defines a culture as distinctly as its language—and the element of language that best encapsulates a society's values and beliefs is its proverbs.

The importance of proverbs in the social interaction of Tibetans is best expressed by one such proverb that says: "Honey is sweet to the mouth; proverb is music to the ear." Many of these sayings, naturally glued to the tongues of many Tibetans, are terse and telling, poetic and pithy, and filled with wit and wisdom. These proverbs also reflect the culture of the Tibetan people, who live in *Gang Jong*, "the Land of Snows," on the highest plateau of the world, and possess a distinctive language, culture, history, and way of life.

There is no doubt that the Tibetan proverbs originated with and developed alongside Tibetan civilization. The earliest written record of Tibetan proverbs can be traced to an ancient manuscript discovered in the Dunhuang caves, which contain scrolls from as long ago as the fourth century C.E. One Tibetan proverb on the scrolls there is this: "Don't break a grateful man's heart; don't break the back of a divine horse."

Many of the proverbs carry two meanings; one literal and the other metaphorical. For instance, "Going up with the steps of a louse, going down with the jump of a musk deer" literally means the pace will be slow while climbing up a mountain and the pace will be much quicker while walking down—but it also refers to the difficulty with which one builds spiritual merit and the comparative ease with which it can be wiped away. Structurally, some Tibetan proverbs are quite poetic and beautifully rhymed, some use simile, and others use personification, and some, like "White is easily blackened; long is easily broken," use double analogy for powerful emphasis.

Until recently many aspects of Tibetan folk literature, though very popular, remained oral or unwritten as the majority of the Tibetan population was illiterate or uneducated—and thus many Tibetan proverbs were preserved only in the minds and stories of Tibetan elders. Nonetheless, it wouldn't be an exaggeration to note that Tibet has actually produced the largest amount of literature, per capita, of any country in the world!

Tibetans have always prized a ready and comprehensive knowledge of proverbs so much that a man possessing such knowledge would be hired by others in his home town as legal representation in courtroom battles. Inside these ancient courts, the case was often won by the representative with the highest powers of persuasion—demonstrated through the skillful deployment of the appropriate proverbs.

My late mother, Dawa, was a treasure trove of Tibetan proverbs—and a wonderful storyteller as well. In our daily conversations she used one proverb after another to make a point or bring home some meaning or lesson, often after she had told me part of the great Tibetan epic tale about King Gesar. I learned many, many proverbs this way. Then, in 1994, I started actively collecting the Tibetan proverbs, noting each down whenever I read or heard one.

Except for a few, I have tried to select those Tibetan proverbs that are not only used in all the three provinces of Tibet but also in the Himalayan regions like Nepal, Bhutan, Sikkim, Spiti, Zanskar, and Ladakh—while at the same time picking the ones likely to resonate in some universal way. When the proverb is more or less self-explanatory, I've let it stand on its own; for other proverbs, I've offered a brief gloss of the meaning or a comment, and in some cases—to point to certain universal themes—I've offered a parallel English-language saying. And in a number of cases, I've taken minor liberties with the English translation to improve readability.

My purpose in presenting this book is twofold: to introduce the wonderful folk wisdom of Tibet to non-Tibetans, and also to encourage and inspire younger Tibetans to acquaint themselves with this unique Tibetan art of expression.

In the process of working on this small book I would like to thank my daughter, Tenzin Dickyi, and my friend Laura Zimmerman for reading the manuscript and helping correct the English renderings of the proverbs.

I'm also grateful to Josh Bartok, senior editor at Wisdom Publications, for his development of the English explanations, and for his meticulous editing. And many thanks to Tim McNeill and Wisdom Publications for bringing out this book.

Pema Tsewang, Shastri

དྲེད་མོས་འཕྱི་བ་བཟུང་བ།

Like a Yeti catching marmots.

The Yeti, or Dremo *in Tibetan, is a dim-witted mythical beast said to feed only on marmots. It sees a marmot, grabs the hapless creature, and then sits on it—saving the delicious morsel for later. And then the Yeti sees another marmot and leaps up to snatch it—while the first marmot makes a quick break for freedom. An image of bumbling, foolish effort—and the pitfalls of greed.*

ཁ་ལ་མངར་མོ་སྒྲང་ཆེ་ཡིན། ཆུ་ལ་སྙན་པོ་གཏམ་དཔེ་ཡིན།

Honey is sweet to the mouth;
proverb is music to the ear.

དཀའ་བའི་བྲག་ལ་མ་ཐུག་ན། བདེ་བའི་སྨྱང་ལ་སྒྲིབས་མི་ཐུབ།

You can't get to the meadow of happiness without climbing the cliff of hardship.

Working through the difficulties in our lives is the only path to contentment.

དཀའ་ལས་སྒྲུབ་བས་བརྒྱབས། ལོངས་སྤྱོད་ཟ་རྒྱས་བཏང་།

It is the spatula that worked hard
but it is the ladle that enjoyed the porridge.

Tibetans make a delicious porridge made from barley, called thugpa. *When being cooked, this porridge must be stirred continuously with a spatula. And then, when it's finally ready, the spatula is put aside and a ladle dips in and serves us the food—and the spatula's hard work is forgotten!*

དཀར་པོ་ནས་ནས། རིང་པོ་ཆས་ནས།

White is easily blackened; long is easily broken.

Akin to "The bigger they are, the harder they fall."

དཀར་ཡོལ་ཆག་ཀྱང་། རི་མོ་བློ་ངེས་ཡིན།

Even though the cup was broken, the pattern lingers in the mind.

This proverb points to the way people and deeds, for instance, live on through their impact on others even after passing away.

འདམ་ཐང་ནང་དུ་རྟ་ཕོའི་ཤེད་ཕྱུགས་རྟོག།

The strength of a horse is known in the marsh.

When we're in a difficult situation, we see who our true friends are—
"A friend in need is a friend indeed."

ཀོང་པ་ཆུ་ལ་མ་རིག་པར། ཉ་མོ་ལག་པས་འཛིན་ཐབས་མེད།།

There is no way to catch a fish by hand without getting one's feet wet.

"You can't make an omelet without breaking some eggs."

རྒྱུན་མ་ནང་ལ་བཞག སྒོ་ལྷག་ཕྱི་ལ་བརྒྱབས།

Locking the door from outside and leaving the thief inside.

"Leaving the fox to stand guard over the henhouse."

ཀྱང་གཅིག་གི་ལྷས་མ། ལག་གཅིག་གི་ཐྭོག་པ།

Knitting with one needle,
clapping with one hand.

This proverb is used akin to two different English proverbs: "Not playing with a full deck" and also "It takes two to tango."

སྐྱྭ་ཀས་སྐྱྭ་ཀར་ཕྱི་རིས་མ་བྱེད། མཆུ་དཀོ་དམར་པོ་འདྲ་འདྲ་རེད།།

A blackbird shouldn't mock another blackbird,
for both have red beaks.

This proverb also evokes two English proverbs:
"That's the pot calling the kettle black"
and
"Those who live in glass houses shouldn't throw stones."

ལྷུག་པས་པས་སྒྲོང་མདོག་བྱས་པ། མངོན་གསལ་ལ་གཞན་ལས་དོད་པ།།

When a fool pretends to be clever,
he looks all the more foolish.

སྐད་གྲགས་ཞེང་གི་ཆེ་ཡང་། ཕན་པོགས་སྒོ་ཁྱི་ཆེ།

Though the lion is more famous,
the dog is more useful.

The Snow Lion, a celestial creature of luminous white fur and a turquoise mane, is the ubiquitous symbol of the Tibetan people. It symbolizes, among other things, fearlessness and unconditional cheerfulness; it appears on Tibet's flag and in countless other places as well. But since it's a mythic being, no one has ever seen one! The tiny Lhasa Apso dog on the other hand—bred for centuries to resemble a miniature Snow Lion—makes an excellent household sentry. Thus, though much less famous, the dog is more useful. It's the common people and everyday things that make the real difference in our lives, not the celebrities.

ཁྱི་ལ་ཞིང་གི་ཏི་ཞིང་བཏགས།

Giving a lion's name to a dog.

"Putting lipstick on pig"—no matter how much you dress it up, it's still a pig; no matter what you call the dog, it's not a lion.

སྐུ་ལུས་གཅིག་ལ་བཀོད་པ་བརྒྱ། ཉི་མ་གཅིག་ལ་འོད་ཟེར་འབྱུམ།

A single body with a hundred manifestations,
a single sun with a hundred thousand rays.

As the sun emits myriad rays to sustain innumerable lives on earth,
so too does a bodhisattva—a transcendent being whose existence
is dedicated to the service of others—manifest in
countless forms to benefit sentient beings.
An image of selfless generosity.

སྐེ་བཅད་ནས་ཚོག་མར་བྱུལ་བྱུལ།

Caressing the chin after cutting the throat.

An insincere or cynically inadequate gesture of apology or restitution.

སྐྲ་འཕྱེར་ནས་ཞགས་པ་བཟེད་པ་དང་། རྫ་འཕྱེར་ནས་རྡོ་ཁ་བ།

Inviting the lasso by sticking out one's neck,
inviting stones by bringing out the earthen-pot.

Asking for trouble—
"The nail that sticks up is the one that is hammered down."

རྒྱ་བ་ལ་འཇམ་པ་དང་། ཐང་ཤིང་ལ་མཛེས་པ།།

Comfortable for the magpie
and beautiful for the pine tree.

Used to describe a win-win situation: The magpie rests comfortably on the branch of the tree, and the tree looks all the more beautiful adorned by the bird.

སྐྱིད་ཀྱི་རྟ་ཐོ་མཉམ་བཞོན། སྡུག་གི་ཁུར་ཐོ་མཉམ་འཁུར།

Ride the horse of happiness together;
bear the load of suffering together.

An expression of a couple who together meet all that life brings,
akin to the traditional wedding vow phrase,
"for richer and for poorer."

རྒྱུད་པོ་རང་གིས་མ་བྱས་ན། སྡུག་པོ་མི་ཡིས་གཉོད་ཉེན་ཡོད།

If you don't make yourself happy,
then others will surely make you suffer.

Not taking responsibility for your own happiness
is the surest path to unhappiness.

སྐྱིད་ཞི་མ་གཏིས་ལ་ཕན་དུས་དང་། ཕྱུག་ལྡན་པ་གཏིས་ལ་ཞེལ་དུས་མེད།།

Happiness and sunshine have no fixed time for occurring;
suffering and darkness have no fixed time for disappearing.

Joys surely come and sorrows surely pass—
but not according to any schedule.

སྒྲུར་མོ་ཞིག་དང་མ་འཕྲད་ན། མངར་མོ་ཐམས་ཅད་ཅང་ཅང་རེད།

If one has not met with sourness,
every sweet thing would taste dull.

Our sorrows enable us to better appreciate life's sweetness;
our enemies help us to appreciate our friends.

སྒྲེས་ཕོ་རབ་གཅིག་གི་ཁོག་པ་ལ། ཚོད་ཐང་དཀར་ལྷོང་བསྐོར་རྒྱག་ས་ཡོད།
སྒྲེས་ཕོ་འབྲིང་གཅིག་གི་ཁོག་པ་ལ། མདའ་གྲི་མདུང་གསུམ་ཤོད་ས་ཡོད།
སྒྲེས་ཕོ་ཐ་ཞིག་གི་ཁོག་པ་ལ། རྒྱ་ཁབ་ཕྱི་མོ་ཐར་ས་མེད།

In the heart of an inferior man, there is not space
even for a needle.
In the heart of a mediocre man, there is space for a spear.
In the heart of a superior man, there is space enough
for an eagle to soar.

The heart of an inferior person is closed and constricted and he cares only for himself; a middling person's heart is a little more accommodative; but a superior person's heart is vast and spacious, open to the entire world.

སྐྱེ་དུས་ཆགས་པ་མི་དྲན། ཆགས་དུས་སྐྱེ་བ་མི་དྲན།

Caught in the pain of giving birth,
one does not remember the desire that led to it;
caught up in desire,
one does not imagine the pain of labor to come.

ཁ་ཁོར་ན་ཕྱིར་འཐེན་བྱེད་ཐབས་མེད། ལམ་ནོར་ན་ཕྱིར་ལོག་བྱེད་ས་ཡོད།

One cannot withdraw what is spoken from one's mouth,
but one can always return back from a mistaken path.

You can't unsay what is said, but it's always possible to make amends.

ཁ་འོ་མ་ཏོག་ཆོར་མ།

Milky mouth, thorny heart.

A person's words may be soft and smooth—
and a deceitful cover of the ill-will within.

ཁ་བཤད་ཆུ་ཡི་ཕྲུ་བ། ལག་ལེན་གསེར་གྱི་ཐིག་པ།

Speech is a water bubble;
implementation is a drop of gold.

It's easy to talk a good game, but really doing it is what matters—
"Walk the walk, don't just talk the talk."

ཁ་གཅིག་ལ་བོད་པ་མི་གཅིག སྤྱས་གཅིག་ལ་རྨི་ལམ་མི་གཅིག།

One mouth, different thoughts;
one pillow, different dreams.

The first part of this proverb refers to the fact that a single person—"one mouth"—may, according to circumstances and conditions and audience, express different and even seemingly contradictory sentiments. The second part refers to the fact that in Tibet, unlike in the West, pillows are large and long enough to accommodate multiple heads at once, such as those of a husband and wife, or of several siblings. But even sharing a pillow thus doesn't mean they will have the same dreams at night.

ཁ་ནང་གི་ཆ་ཁ་ནང་དུ་གསོ་དགོས།

The wound within the mouth must be healed inside the mouth.

This proverb is used akin to "Don't air your dirty laundry in public"—settle private matters privately.

ཁ་ཟས་སྨྲང་ནས་བཟས། རིལ་མ་ནགས་སུ་བཏང་།།

Eating grass from the pasture
but carrying one's dung to the forest.

Dung is, of course, excellent fertilizer that could help a pasture grow lush. This image is one of using resources in one place but returning the beneficial "fruit" elsewhere.

ཁམ་བུ་བཟའ་འདོད་མེད་པར། སྐྱེད་ཁ་སྐྱུར་ལ་བཏགས།

While not wanting to eat a peach,
the pretext was put on its sourness.

Though often associated with warm climates, the peach is actually quite common in Tibet, especially in the provinces of Lhasa and Kongpo, for instance. This is an image of giving spurious excuses to justify what you've already decided you want to do.

ཁོང་ཁྲོ་སྐྱེད་མཁན་མེད་ན། བཟོད་པ་སྒྲུབ་ལ་སྐྱོན།

When there is no one to provoke anger,
how shall we practice patience?

It's only our seeming adversaries who give us the opportunity to develop the virtue of patience; if everything always went our way and everyone always did or said exactly what we'd wish, we'd have no cause to refine our character and develop wholesome qualities.

ཁོང་ཁྲོ་ལྟ་བའི་སྡུག་བསྔལ་མེད། བཟོད་པ་ལྟ་བའི་དཀའ་ཐུབ་མེད།

There is no suffering like anger;
there is no penance like patience.

Anger is it's own punishment,
and patience is its own reward.

ཁོང་ཁྲོ་གཡག་ལ་ཟ། རྟ་ཀུག་རྡེལ་ལ་གཞུས།

Angry at the yak but kicking the mule.

An image of displaced anger that erupts in inappropriate or undeserved places.

ཁོ་གཱ་ནང་དུ་མེ་འབར་ཡང། དུ་བ་ཁ་ནས་མ་བཏོན།

Even though your heart burns,
don't let smoke come out of your mouth.

Sometimes it's best to just keep your mouth shut—
no matter how angry or hurt you may feel.

ཁྱོད་ཀྱིས་ལམ་ལ་བསྐྱོད་པ་ལས། ང་ཡིས་ཟམ་པ་བརྒལ་བ་མང་།

I have crossed more bridges than you have walked on the road.

Akin to expressions like "I have more experience in my little finger than you do in your entire life." It also refers to the worldly experience gained in travel.

ཁྲིམས་ཀྱིས་བསྡམས་ན་བཀྲ་དང་། ཐག་པས་བསྡམས་ན་གཅིག།

A law binds hundreds of people;
a rope binds just one.

An image of casting too wide a net; making an onerous law binding everyone, when just "tying up" the lone transgressor would be more sensible.

ལག་པས་ཁེས་ཡོན་རྡོར་ལ་བརྟེ། གྲྭན་པས་གསེར་དངུལ་རྡོར་ལ་བརྟེ།

The foolish think riches are gold and silver;
the wise know that learning is wealth.

མཁས་ཀྱང་དོན་ལ་མ་དཔྱད་ན། ས་འོག་གསེར་གྱི་མདངས་དང་འདྲ།

Even to a wise man, meaning that is not studied
is like the light of buried gold.

Akin to Socrates's statement that
"The unexamined life is not worth living."
Also: even the wise must study and
work to refine their wisdom.

གང་ལ་དགའ་ན་དེ་ལ་མཁས།

One becomes skilled in what one likes.

གོམ་གཅིག་མ་སྟོས་གྲོང་བཞི་མི་འགོར།
ཆུ་ཐིགས་མ་བསགས་རྒྱ་མཚོ་མི་ཡོང་།

One cannot reach four corners of the world
unless one makes the first step;
the ocean is not possible without
the collection of water drops.

"A journey of a thousand miles begins with a single step"—
and great deeds are accomplished bit by bit.

གོས་ཆེན་ཐོག་ལ་འཚེམ་དྲུབ། རལ་བའི་ཐོག་ལ་ལྷན་པ།

Embroidery upon brocade,
a patch upon a rip.

A phrase contrasting unnecessary embellishment on something already beautiful with a simple and necessary fix.

གྱེན་རེ་འཛོགས་ན་ཐུར་རེ་ཡོད།

Every incline has a decline.

"What goes up must come down."

གྲོག་མ་ལས་ལ་རྟོལ་བ་དེ། རྟ་ཐོག་མི་ཡིས་ག་ལ་མཐོང་།

How can the man on the horse see
the ant struggling for survival?

"You can't truly know another's difficulties until you've walked a mile in his shoes, and you know for yourself where the shoe pinches." Everyone has difficulties in life, we just don't always see them.

ཐོ་གས་པོས་བསྒྲ་དུས་དགོ་བཞིན་བསྒྲ། ཁམ་པས་བསྒྲ་དུས་ཏ་བཞིན་བསྒྲ།

Some deceive you with a smile;
others deceive you by weeping.

Seeming kind, one "friend" may use flattery to manipulate and deceive, another may weep "crocodile tears," making a grand display of insincere feeling. Also used to remind us to beware getting too caught up in others' reactions—or in our own!

གློས་མི་ལ་དྲིས། ཐག་རང་གིས་གཅོད།

Ask others for suggestions,
make the decision yourself.

མགོ་སྒྲུ་མེད་ལ་རལ་པའི་ཁྲལ།

The bald man having to pay a tax on braids.

An image of bearing a burden but reaping no benefit.

མགོ་རིལ་རིལ་ཐམས་ཅད་དགེ་སློང་དང་།

ལུས་སེར་སེར་ཐམས་ཅད་བླ་མ་མིན།

All with shaved heads are not monks;
all with saffron robes are not lamas.

"All that glitters is not gold"—
especially when it comes to people.

འགྲོ་ཞིང་ན་ཆུ་སྦ་བཏོལ་འདྲ་དགོས། སྡོད་ཞིང་ན་རྒྱ་མཚོ་འཁྲིལ་འདྲ་དགོས།

Going forth, be like water bursting out;
staying at rest, be like the calm sea.

When you do something, really do it wholeheartedly;
when you cease, really let it go.

ཆོད་པོ་འཁྲིད་ན་མཐུར་མདའ་རིང་དགོས།
ཤོང་ཆེན་གཅོད་ན་ས་ཡུ་རིང་དགོས།

One needs a long rein to lead an untamed horse; one needs an axe with a long handle to chop down an ancient tree.

To control the strong-willed, sometimes one needs to take a few steps back and give them more space.

རྒྱགས་དུས་ཆོས་དན། ལྷོགས་དུས་རྒྱ་དན།

One thinks of Dharma when the stomach is full;
one thinks of stealing when the stomach is empty.

It's easy to think holy thoughts in comfort and privilege,
but doing so in hardship too is the real test.

སྒོ་ངའི་ནང་གི་ཕེར་རིལ། ཙ་ཡོད་ནང་གི་ད་ཡོད།

The yolk from the egg, the best among those present.

Tibetans regard the yolk as the "essence" of the egg, and the most tasty part—this image is akin to "the cream of the crop."

སྒོ་གཡ་ལ་བཟས་ཀྱང་། སྒོ་ཏི་ངོས་ལ་ཀ་བ།།

The smell of garlic can be sniffed from afar
even though the garlic was eaten in secrecy.

You can hide the deed but not the consequences.

སྒྲོན་མེ་འོད་གསལ་ཡང་། རང་གི་ཞབས་རས་མི་མཐོང་།

Even though the lamp is bright,
it cannot see beneath its own base.

Even the wisest have their blind spots.

བགད་དེ་བརྒྱ་ཐུབ། ཁྲོས་ཏེ་གཅིག་མི་ཐུབ།

A smile wins a hundred hearts;
a frown not even one.

ངོ་བསྟོད་ཀྱིས་གཉེན་མི་འགྱོངས། ཚིག་རྩུབ་ཀྱིས་དགྲ་མི་འགྱལ།

Praise alone will not sustain friends;
harsh words cannot vanquish foes.

Akin to "Action speaks louder than words"
or "Fine words butter no parsnips."

རྡུ་ཚིགས་ལ་དཔག་པའི་ཞབས་བྲོ་རྒྱུག།

One must dance according to the beats of the drum.

Akin to both "When in Rome, do as the Romans do" and "You've got to play the game with the cards you're dealt."

སྦུར་དུག་སྦྲུལ་ནས་པོས་སྟོག་བཙད། ད་ཕ་ཀུ་ཐུར་ཐུར་ཡིད་མི་ཆེས།།

Once frightened by a poisonous snake,
now one fears even a striped rope.

An image of overgeneralized anxiety—"Once bitten, twice shy."

གཅན་གཟན་གྱིས་ཀྱང་རང་རྒྱུད་མི་བཟ།

Even the wild animals do not eat one of their own.

Akin to "There is honor among thieves."

ལྷག་ཚ་ཐོག་ལ་རྡུངས། ཀོ་བ་རྒྱོན་ཐོག་ལ་མཉེད།།

Hit the iron when it's hot;
cure the leather when it's wet.

The first part of this proverb has an almost exact parallel in English: "Strike while the iron is hot."

ལྷང་མར་ལྷང་སྒྲོར་མ་ཐུབ་རུང་། ལྷང་རྩ་རྡོ་ཡིས་རྡུང་མི་ཅེན།

Even if you can't build a fence to protect the sapling, at least avoid stacking stones on its roots.

Even if you can't help, at least do less harm.

བཅད་པའི་ཕྲུལ་ལ་བཙོག་པ་འདྲ་བ།

Stabbed on the same spot where the cut was.

"Rubbing salt in the wound" or reawakening past hurts.

ཆས་སྨོ་བྱུང་ན་འགོ་དང་། ཟུ་གི་བྱུང་ན་མཐའ།

Disaster strikes at the top; famine strikes at the bottom.

Here disaster *refers mainly to the problems thought about by leaders and people in charge—like, for instance, a precipitous fall in the exchange rate of a country's currency. Such things are not generally the concern of the general populace. But such troubles like famine—when basic resources are themselves very scarce—are mainly felt by the common person, and a nation's elite will rarely be the first to go unnourished.*

ཆགས་པར་ཕན་ཡང་། ཡ་མར་གཙོ་ད།།

That which cures the cold inflames the sinus.

Sometimes the medicine can be as bad as the affliction.
Also akin to "Out of the frying pan, into the fire."

ཆང་ལན་ཆུ་འད�། བཟང་ལན་ངན་འདEL།

Repaying water for wine
and cruelty for kindness.

Images of ingratitude and unequal consideration.

ཆུ་དགོས་ནས་མར་མི་འཐོན། རྡོ་གཡམ་བཅོར་ནས་སྦྱུམ་མི་ལོན།

You can't make butter by churning water;
you can't get oil by squeezing slate.

Some things are just impossible—
"You can't squeeze blood from a stone."

ཆུ་ལ་རྒྱུག་པ་གཞུས་ནས། ཉ་ལ་ལྷོ་ཡང་མེད།

You can beat the lake with a stick,
but it won't matter to the fish.

An image of ineffectual aggression—like "spitting into the wind."
Also an image for angry words or deeds
that roll off someone "like water off a duck's back."

ཆུ་ཆར་བའི་སྒྲོར་རོགས་མ་བྱུང་ཡང་། སད་ས་བའི་ས་འདྲེན་མ་བྱེད།

Don't call down hail, even if you can't summon rain.

This proverb comes from the belief that certain great yogis can develop supernatural powers—even going so far as to be able to influence the weather! Accordingly, this proverb says that if you can't helpfully summon nourishing rain, you should at least refrain from causing devastating hail.

ཆུ་བོ་ཆུང་ཆུང་འདུར་སྒྲ་ཆེ། ཡོན་ཏན་ཆུང་ཆུང་ང་རྒྱལ་ཆེ།

A small stream makes more sound; fools are the ones who brag.

Akin to Plato's statement: "As empty vessels make the loudest sound, so they that have the least wit are the greatest babblers."

ཆུ་འཚོག་པའི་སྣོད་ཡོད་ཀྱང་། གཏམ་འཚོག་པའི་སྣོད་མེད།

There are vessels that can capture water
but none that can capture words.

Water can be caught and contained,
but nothing can stop the spread of gossip.

གནམ་ལ་རོག་རྒྱག་གཞུས་ན། ལྷག་ཐུང་རོ་ལ་བརྡབ་ཡོང་།

If you try to kick the sky,
you'll only hit the back of your head on the ground
(when you fall over backward).

Images of ineffectuality, especially ineffectual anger—
and also akin to "Spitting into the wind."

ཆུ་ཆུང་དུས་ཆུ་རགས་མ་བརྒྱབས་ན། ལུང་ཆུང་ཆུ་ཡིས་འཁྱེར་ཏེ་ཡོད།
མེ་ཆུང་དུས་མེ་སྐྱགས་མ་བསད་ན། ནགས་སྐྱ་ཙོ་མེ་ཡིས་འཚོག་ཏེ་ཡོད།

If the dike is not built when the water is low,
the valley may be flooded.
If the fire is not extinguished when the ember is tiny,
the thick forests may be lost to fire.

It's essential to take action at the first sign of a problem.
"A stitch in time saves nine."

ཆོག་ཤེས་ལྡན་ན། རྩོར་ལ་མང་ཉུང་མེད།

If one possesses contentment,
less or more wealth makes no difference.

ཀུན་དང་མཐུན་པ་མི་ཚེས་རྒྱ་ཡིན།

To live in harmony is the essence of human morality.

In the Tibetan culture, so deeply influenced for centuries by Buddhism, morality is not found in the adherence to rules as such, but rather through living harmoniously with each other and the world.

ཆོས་མི་ལ་བྱོད་པར། རང་ཉིད་ཐོམ་པ་གཙང་དགོས།།

In order to teach Dharma to others,
one needs to have a pure morality.

In Tibetan Buddhism, the most important quality a guru must possess is a capacity to act unfailingly in keeping with the highest ethical standards, the moral precepts of Buddhism. Without that, a teacher is not truly teaching Dharma.

ཇ་ཚ་མེད་དང་གཏམ་འཆོ་མེད།

Tea without salt,
speech without meaning.

Traditionally, the Tibetans add salt to their tea, and to them that is what makes tea delicious and worth drinking. Tea without salt is an image of hollow or empty words.

འཇའ་ཁ་དོག་མཚར་ཀྱང་སྙིང་པོ་མེད།

Even though the colors of rainbows are wonderful, they are essenceless.

Superficial attractiveness in itself serves no real function. Also a reminder that, in the words of the Heart Sutra, "form is emptiness."

བྱས་དཔོན་མང་ན་བྱས་ཉེས་ཤོར།

Too many strategists make the plan fail.

"Too many cooks spoil the broth."

ཐྲོ་ན་ཤིང་སྐམ་པོར་འབྲས་བུའི་རེ་བ་མེད།

You can't expect fruit from a dried plant.

An image of something that just isn't going to happen.

ཉ་བས་ནས་ཁྱི་ལ་སྲོན་པ་བཏང་།

Killing the fish to feed the dog.

Akin to "Robbing Peter to pay Paul."

ཙ་མཆོག་བཀོག་ནས། ཀུད་ཀྱི་ལྟན་པ།

Patching one's ass by cutting off one's ear.

An image for something that fixes one problem by causing another, such as trying to mend a robe by cutting off its sleeve to make a patch.

ཉལ་བ་ལ་ཆུ་མ་མང་། ཤི་བ་ལ་བ་མ་མང་།

Don't drink too much before sleeping;
don't talk too much before dying.

In ancient Tibet there were hardly any indoor toilets and so people had to get up and go outside into the frigid air to ease themselves in the middle of night—so drinking too much before bed was a very bad idea. Similarly, even on your deathbed it's important to be especially mindful of how you use your speech.

ཉི་འོད་སྒྲར་མོས་མི་ཁེབས།

Sunshine cannot be blocked by a hand.

A truly good deed or manifest wholesome benefit cannot be besmirched even by lies, rumors, or half-truths.

གཉིད་མ་ཉལ་གོང་ལ་རྨི་ལམ་བཤད།

Telling the dream before one has slept.

Akin to "counting the chickens before they're hatched."

གཏམ་ལ་ཆོ་ངར་མེད་ཀྱང་། མི་སྙིང་དུམ་བུར་གཏུབས།

Even though harsh speech has no sharp edge,
it can cut the human heart to pieces.

རྟ་ཁོད་པོ་ཕོར་ན་འཇོན་ཐབས་ཡོད།
ཚིག་ཁོད་པོ་ཕོར་ན་འཇོན་ཐབས་མེད།

A wild horse can be caught if it escapes;
a harsh word cannot be caught if it escapes.

Be careful with your speech—something said in the heat of anger cannot be unsaid.

རྒ་ཆེན་ཆས་བཅོས་བྱས་པ་ངན་ལ་མངོན།
ཕག་པ་དོང་གསོས་བརྒྱབས་པ་བཟང་པོར་མངོན།

An old horse, treated for its back sore, considers it as torture;
a pig, well fed for its meat, considers it as kindness.

Sometimes what seems like cruelty is kindness
and sometimes what seems like kindness is not.

སྟག་ལ་མཆོངས་ཆེན་བཅོ་བརྒྱད་ཡོད་ན། ཁ་ལ་འཕྲལ་ཁུང་བཅུ་དགུ་ཡོད།

If the tiger has eighteen great leaps,
the fox has nineteen hiding holes.

An image of being well-prepared for all eventualities.

བརྟན་པོས་བསྒྲས་པ་གང་ཡང་མེད།

Caution has betrayed no one.

Akin to Shakespeare's "The better part of valor is discretion."

ཐྭག་ཁོག་གཅིག་ལ་ཟར་བུ་གཉིས། གྲི་ཤུབས་གཅིག་ལ་སྒྲ་ཐང་གཉིས།།

One pot with two ladles, one sheath with two swords.

Two ladles get in each other's way; two swords won't fit in the same sheath. Also, akin to the Biblical saying that "You can't serve two masters."

ཐོས་པ་བརྒྱ་ལས། མཐོང་བ་གཅིག་ལྷག

Seeing once is far better than hearing one hundred times.

"A picture is worth a thousand words."

མཐོ་ན་དགའ་སྟེ། དམའ་ན་བརྟན།།

Though it is better to be higher, it is more stable to be lower.

"Uneasy lies the head that wears the crown."

དར་དུས་དགྲ་ཡང་གཉེན། གྲོང་དུས་གཉེན་ཡང་དགྲ

When prosperous, even enemies become friends;
when poor, even relatives turn into enemies.

When things are going well for you it's easy to collect hangers-on, but when the storm comes you are often abandoned even by those who should be closest.

དཀ་སྦྱོལ་ཡིན་པའི་རྟེས་ལ། ཕ་སྦོམ་གང་ལ་ཁྱད་མེད།

If the snake is poisonous,
it does not matter whether it is thick or thin.

Sometimes knowing details is not relevant to the matter at hand.

བདེན་པ་མར་ཡིན་ཡང་མི་བཞུ། རྫུན་མ་ལྷགས་ཡིན་ཡང་མཐེལ་བརྩོལ།

If truth were butter, it wouldn't melt;
if lies were iron, they would still break.

Truth has value, weight, and intrinsic durability,
whereas even the best lie is fragile and worthless.

མདའ་གཅིག་གིས་ཤ་བ་གཉིས་བསད།

Killing two deer with one arrow.

"Killing two birds with one stone."

འདྲིས་ཆེ་ན་ཞིང་གི་ཁྱི་ཡིས་རྒྱལ་པ། ཐག་ཏེ་ན་མིག་གིས་ཐྲི་མ་མི་མཐོང་།།

Too much familiarity makes a dog bite a lion;
too much intimacy makes the eyes overlook eyelashes.

Akin to "Familiarity breeds contempt"—and also a reminder that we tend to overlook the needs of those closest to us.

འདོད་པས་ངོ་ཚ་བཟློག་པས།

Desire eclipses decency.

རྡོ་ཆུང་ཡང་རྫུ་བཅོག་ མེ་ཆུང་ཡང་སྐྲ་འཚོག།

However small a stone may be, it can break a pot;
however small a fire may be, it can singe your hair.

Small things can still have an impact.

ནད་པ་རྒད་པོ་ཨེམ་རྗེ་ཡིན།

An old patient is a doctor.

Our experience—especially of hardship—makes us wise and able to be of service to others.

རྒྱོ་བྱ་ལག་ཏུ་ཡོད་དུས་རྒྱོ་ཉམས་མ་ཆོད།

When the jewel was in hand,
its worth was not recognized.

"You don't know what you've got 'till it's gone."

ཁེ་ཙོ་སྨྲ་བས་གཟིབ་ཏུ་ཚུད། འདབ་ཆགས་ལྷུགས་པ་བདེ་བར་ཆུ།།

The parrot is caged because it can talk;
other birds move freely because they cannot.

Sometimes it's being too special that gets us into trouble.

པུས་མོ་བཙུགས་ནས་གསོན་པ་ལས། ཡང་པོར་ལངས་ནས་ཤི་ན་དགའ།

Better to die on your feet than to live on your knees.

དཔའ་དུས་དགོན་ལ་ཡ་བོ་བཟུང་། ལྷར་དུས་ཁྱི་ལ་ཕྱག་འདུལ་ཞུ།

The brave challenge authority;
the cowardly salute even a dog.

སྒྲ་པའི་ཞིང་ལ་སྒྲར་གྱི་ཐོང་གཤོལ་བཙུགས།

To use a personal plow on the public field.

"Dipping your pen in the company ink."

སྨྱོ་ཤེས་ནད་དག་ཀྱང་སྨན་དུ་གྱུར།

Even poison can be turned into medicine if one knows how to use it.

What's harmful to some in some circumstances can be beneficial to others in other circumstances. One traditional Tibetan image is that of a peacock that can eat from a grove of poisonous plants and transform the plants into beautiful plumage—similarly, through training the mind we can use our anger and grasping as fuel for developing kindness and wisdom.

ཕ་སྤུན་དགྲ་ལ་ལངས་ཀྱང་། རུས་པ་གསེར།

Even though one's relatives rose up as enemies,
their bones are as dear as gold.

We may fight with our relatives all our lives, but it's best to remember only the good when they've died—and even in life, amid struggle, the blood connection still remains.

ཕག་པས་བལ্�་ན། ཕག་ཚང་གཞལ་ཡས་ཁང་།

A pig sees its own sty as a divine abode.

ཕག་པས་གནམ་མཁའ་བ་དུས་གཅིག་ཡིན།

A pig sees the sky only once.

Images of shortsighted ignorance and complacent contentment with worldly circumstances at the cost of spiritual development—the truth and true cost of which only become clear at the time of death.

ཕར་ཕོད་གྱི་མི་ལ་ཚུར་ཡོད་གྱི་གཏམ།

A man who makes a journey has a story when he returns.

ཕོ་རབ་གཏམ་གྱིས་བསླུས། ཕོ་འབྲིང་རྒྱ་ཡིས་བསླུས།
ཕོ་ཐ་ཟས་ཀྱིས་བསླུས།

A superior man is deceived by speech;
a middling man is deceived by wealth;
a lowly man is deceived by food.

It takes a fine argument to deceive a superior man, a middling one assumes that wealth goes along with righteousness, and a fool will believe anything if it comes with a moment of satisfaction.

ཕོ་རབ་ཀྱི་གཏམ་དེ་མགོ་དུས་ཚགས། ཕོ་འབྲིང་གི་གཏམ་དེ་འདྲི་དུས་ཚགས།
ཕོ་ཐ་མའི་གཏམ་དེ་རྒྱབ་ཏུ་ཚགས།

A superior man talks when required;
a middling man talks when asked;
a lowly man talks when the back is turned.

Speech is powerful—but wisdom is often expressed in silence. The wise use speech when necessary, the middling when invited, and the lowly gossip wantonly.

ཕ་རབ་རྣོད་ཀྱི་སྟེ་བྱེད། ཕ་འབྲིང་རྣོད་ཀྱི་རང་བྱུས། ཕ་ཐ་རྣོད་ཀྱི་ཁ་ཕོར།

A superior man argues for communal welfare;
a middling man argues for self-interest;
a lowly man argues for his own bowl.

A wise person looks to the good of all, a middling one only to his ultimate self-interest, and a lowly person looks no further than immediate gratification.

ཁོ་རང་ཚོད་ཟིན་ན་རྒྱལ་པོ་དང་། ཟས་ཟ་ཚོད་ཟིན་ན་སྨན་པ་ཡིན།

He who can control himself is a king;
he who can limit his diet is a doctor.

Self-restraint is the highest freedom and the best medicine.

བོང་བུ་བཞོན་ནས། བོང་བུ་འཚོལ་བ།

Looking for the donkey while riding on it.

Akin to "He couldn't find the nose on his face."

བྱ་མ་འདྲོགས་པར། ཐྭོ་ང་ལོན་ཟབས།

Snatching the egg without frightening the hen.

An image of effective effort, requiring delicacy and skill.

བློན་པོས་བསྟོད་པ་ལས། མཁས་པས་སྨད་པ་དགའ།

It is better to be denounced by the wise than praised by fools.

Even the censure of wise people can be put to good use if we let it alter our unwholesome behavior—but even praise from fools is unhelpful.

བླུན་པོས་བོར་ན་གཅིག་བོར། མཁས་པས་བོར་ན་བརྒྱ་བོར།

A mistake committed by a fool is one mistake;
a mistake committed by a wise man is hundreds of mistakes.

When teachers or other people in respected roles of leadership make mistakes, the consequences multiply because so many people look to them for guidance and example. No one looks to a fool for such things.

ཤིང་ལས་བྱས་པའི་སེང་གེ་དེ། འཇིགས་འཇིགས་འདྲ་ཡང་སྙིང་པོ་མེད།

A lion made from wood, though impressive, is devoid of essence.

A "paper tiger"—someone or something that appears powerful but has nothing behind the appearance.

དབུལ་པོ་ལ་རྒྱུ་ཡོད་ན། ཕྱུག་པོ་གཉིད་མི་ཞུག

When a poor man possesses wealth the rich man can't sleep.

Akin to Gore Vidal's comment: "It's not enough that I succeed—others must fail."

སྦ་ལ་པ་རྒྱ་ཅན་གཅིག་གིས་སྦ་ལ་ཆོང་ཕྲུང་།

One sick frog will destroy a whole colony of frogs.

"One bad apple spoils the barrel."

སྦ་ལ་པ་མཐོང་དུས། ཅོང་མོ་སངས་རྒྱས་རེད།

When one sees the toad, the tadpole is a Buddha.

Though not beautiful by any stretch of the imagination,
compared to the ugliness of a full-grown toad,
a tadpole can seem much more appealing—
if only because it's smaller.
Used in circumstances where one might say in English
that someone or something is "the lesser of two evils."

འབྲུག་སྒྲ་ཆེ་ལ་ཆར་ཐག་གྱང་།

Great thunder and only brief rain.

All talk and little action; all style and little substance.

མ་འགྱུར་ན་བློ་མིན། མ་ཁྲུག་ས་ན་སེམས་མིན།

An unchanging mind is not a mind;
an unforgiving heart is not a heart.

If you're incapable of changing your mind when necessary, you're a fool.
If you're incapable of forgiveness, you may as well be heartless.

མང་པོའི་དཀྱིལ་དུ་ཁ་ལ་བརྟག གཅིག་ཏུར་སྟོད་དུས་ཞེམས་ལ་བརྟག

Examine your speech when in public;
examine your mind when alone.

Be careful what you say when around others;
be careful what you think by yourself.

མི་ཁེམས་གཅིག་ཏུ་བསྡོམ་ན། རི་རྒྱལ་ལྷུན་པོ་སྟོ་ཐུབ།

If all the minds of men were united,
they could move even Mount Meru from its place.

According to Buddhist cosmology, Mount Meru (also known as Mount Sumeru) is a vast mountain in the center of the world—but even such a great mountain is no match for unity of will. Also akin to "Many hands make light work."

མི་བོད་མིས་མི་ལོངས། རྡོ་བོ་ཆུ་ཡིས་མི་ལོངས།

The depth of one human heart cannot be understood by another;
the core of a stone cannot be plumbed by water.

An image of the difficulty of ever really knowing another person's heart.

མི་ཡུལ་འོད་ཀྱིས་བརྒྱངས། རང་ཡུལ་སྟོང་པར་བཞག།

Illuminating another's country, leaving one's own dark.

Caring about those afar while ignoring those nearest by.

མི་མང་ཁ་དེ་དུག་ཡིན། མི་མང་ལག་པ་གསེར་ཡིན།

The mouths of the many are poison;
the hands of the many are gold.

When a group of people stands idly by caught up in gossip, much harm is done; but when they join together in common purpose, much good can be accomplished.

མི་ཆེན་པའི་ཁ་ལ་ཉོན། ཏྲ་གཞོན་པའི་སྐྲ་ལ་ལྟོས།

Listen to the advice of old people;
look to the feathers of young birds.

Of birds, the young ones have the prettier feathers;
of people, the old ones, because they're more experienced and wiser,
give the better advice.

མེ་དུ་བ་མེད་པར་གཏོང་མི་ཉེས། ཆུ་རྩྭངས་པ་མེད་པར་སྐོལ་མི་ཉེས།

You cannot make a fire without smoke;
you cannot boil water without steam.

མེ་འབར་བའི་སྟོང་དུ་ཤིང་ཕན་པ།

Adding pieces of wood to the burning fire.

Akin to "Adding insult to injury" and also an image of "Fanning the flames" of discord.

ཨ་བྱ་དང་ཁྭ་ཀ་མི་འགྲོགས། ཟླང་ཆེན་དང་བ་ཟླང་མི་སྡེབ།

A peacock and a crow are never friends;
an elephant and a cow never mate.

"Oil and water never mix."

ཚན་དན་ཤིག་པའི་ཀ་བ་གཅིས། མདུང་མ་འདེགས་པའི་ནུས་པ་མཚུངས།

The pillar made of sandalwood and
the pillar made of cypress offer equal support to the beam.

Sometimes all that matters is that a thing gets done,
regardless of how or by whom.

ཙན་དན་གྱི་གུ་གཡོག གོས་ཆེན་གྱི་ཐབ་ཕྱེས།

Sandalwood as kindling, brocade as the kitchen mop.

Images of wasted finery—
"Like throwing pearls before swine."

ཙི་ཙི་མ་མས་གྲོས་བྱས་ནས། ཞུམ་བྱའི་སྐྱེ་ལ་གཡེར་ཀ་གཡོགས།

Putting a bell on the cat's neck
after the mother of mice was consulted.

This refers to a story about a wise mother-mouse who, in a wily effort to help protect her children, tells the cat that the mice wish to award him a medal for bravery and cleverness. The cat is only too pleased to be so honored, and so the mice carefully place the award—a loud, tinkling bell—around the cat's neck. An image of the immutability of self-interest and the foolishness of vanity.

རྩིས་པའི་བ་བརྒྱགས། ཨེམ་རྗེའི་མ་གྲོངས།

Even the astrologer's cow gets lost;
even the doctor's mother dies.

There are some things forever beyond even a master's control—
"Time and tide wait for no man."

ཚོང་པས་བསམ་རྒྱ་ཁེ་བཟང་། ཞུམ་བུས་བསམ་རྒྱ་ཅི་ཅི།

A businessman only thinks of profit;
a cat only thinks of mice.

ཚིག་རྩུབ་སྨྲ་བའི་གྲོགས་པོ་དེ། ཤ་ཚ་སྙིང་ནས་བྱེད་པའི་རྟགས།

A friend who expresses harsh words loves you from the heart.

Good friends will tell you the truth—
even if the truth sometimes hurts.

མཚོ་ནང་རྒྱ་མཚའི་ཟླ་སྐར་ཀུན། གསལ་ཡང་རང་གི་གཏིང་མི་མཐོང་།

Even though all the reflections of moon and stars appear in the sea, the sea cannot see its own depth.

Even though it is easy to see others' faults and strong qualities, it's difficult to see one's own.

གཞན་གྱི་སྡུག་བསྔལ་སེལ་བ་དེ། དམ་པའི་ཆོས་ཀྱི་སྙིང་པོ་ཡིན།

Eliminating the suffering of others is the essence of the sublime Dharma.

In Buddhism, bodhicitta, *the heartfelt aspiration to save and serve all other beings, is the most important personal quality we can cultivate.*

ཟས་ཞིམ་པོ་ཚོ་ཐེངས་གཅིག གཏམ་མི་ཁ་བསླ་ལ་པ་སྟོང་།

Delicious food lasts for just one meal;
a bad reputation lasts for thousands of eons.

ག
্ལགས་མེད་གྲིབ་བཟོ་དང་། ཉེས་མེད་ཉེས་འདོགས།

Creating a shadow without any form,
leveling an accusation without any crime.

"Rasing waves where there is no wind"—
an image of manufacturing harmful lies.

བཟང་པོའི་ལས་དེ་འགྱངས་མི་རྒྱང་། ངན་པའི་གཏམ་དེ་ཟོད་མི་རྒྱང་།

Helpful action shouldn't be put off;
harmful words shouldn't be spoken.

རང་སྙོང་དབང་འདྲུས། གཞན་སྙོང་ཟེལ་གྱིས་གཏོན།

He who conquers himself,
conquers all.

རིག་རྩལ་སྦྱང་ལ་མི་ཤོར། བརྩོན་འགྲུས་རྡོ་ལ་ཞེ་ཁྱང་ཕྱག

Cleverness is like a fire ripping through the pasture and perseverance is like piercing a hole in the rock.

Some virtues are flashy and dramatic, like wildfire in a field,
others are slow, subtle, and much harder to see—
like eons of dripping water eroding a hole in a rock—
but just as powerful.
An image encouraging persistent and diligent effort.

གཡུ་ཐུ་རུ་ཡོད་དུས་སྨོས་ཤེལ་བོར།

Throwing away the amber stone when turquoise and ruby become available.

Leaving an old friend when a new, more impressive or famous one is around.

ལག་པ་ལ་ཤ་ཡོད་ན། རྒྱ་མཁན་ལ་བྱ་ལྟེང་།

Vultures gather when there is meat in one's hand.

And "friends" flock to you when you have something they want.

ལོ་བརྒྱ་སྨན་དང་། འཆི་ཁར་དུག

Medicine for one hundred years and poison at the time of death.

The worldly pleasures that we may spend our life pursuing cannot save us or comfort us when it comes time to die—and the more attachment we've cultivated in our lifetime, the more painful it all is to lose.

ཤ་ཆ་བའི་ཚོག་དེ་སྨན་པོ་མེད། རང་མཁྱེས་པའི་སྒྲན་དེ་ཞིམ་པོ་མེད།

Medicine for jaundice is not sweet;
words spoken out of love are not music to the ear.

Traditional Tibetan medicine can effectively treat the symptoms of jaundice—but the concoction used to do it is very bitter and unpleasant to drink.
"Sometimes the truth is a bitter pill to swallow"—sometimes it's painful to hear what needs to be said.

ཤ་བ་ར་ཅོ་རིང་ཡང། གནམ་གྱི་སྐས་ཀ་མི་ཡོང།

Even though the antlers of deer are long,
they cannot become ladders to the sky.

The use of this proverb is akin to the saying that "When all you have is a hammer, the whole world looks like a nail." Though a certain trait may be good to have, it is nonetheless not a panacea.

ཤེས་གསོད་པར་སྣ་རེ་འཕྱར་མི་དགོས།

There is no need to wield an axe to kill a louse.

An image of overkill—
like trying to use a fire-hose as a water fountain.

ཤིག་དང་འཇེ་བ་སྨོ་མ་གསུམ། ཆོ་སྨོག་དོར་ས་ཐེན་མོའི་སྟེང་།

The flea, louse, and nit each die
under the fingernails.

In Tibet, pests like fleas, lice, and nits are killed by being crushed between the thumbnails—though each is different, the way they die is the same. Similarly, in the greatest matters of life and death, the differences among us—our appearance, our job, our relative wealth—are ultimately of no significance.

ཤིང་དགྲ་སྟ་རེ་ཡིན་ཝོད་ཀྱང་། དེ་ཡི་ཡུ་བ་ཤིང་གིས་བྱེད།

Even though the axe is the tree's natural enemy,
its handle is still made from wood.

Sometimes in order to function properly in the world,
we are dependent even upon the existence of our enemies.

སང་ཉིན་གྱི་ཤ་ལས། དེ་རིང་གི་རུས་པ་ཞིམ།

Today's bone is more delicious than tomorrow's meat.

"A bird in hand is worth two in the bush."

ཕྱི་གསར་པ་ལས། འདྲེ་ཁྱོང་པ་དགའ།

An old demon is better than a new deity.

"It's better to dance with the devil you know than an angel you don't"—because you never know what's hiding behind an angel's mask.

ལྷན་སྐྱེས་ཡོན་ཏན་མེད་གྱུར་ན། ཕྱི་ཚུལ་བཅོས་པས་ཅི་ལ་ཕན།

If one does not have an inherent quality,
external pretension is of no help.

Akin to the opposite meaning of
"Clothes make the man."

ཚོ་ལོ་དང་གོས་ཆུང་ཚད་ཀྱིན་ཚད་ཀྱིན།

One needs to adjust the clothing to suit to the child.

In so many of life's situations, there is no one-size-fits-all solution.

ཞ་མའི་བུ་ལ་ཡོན་ཏན་ཡོད་ན། དགའ་ལྡན་ཁྲི་ལ་དམ་ཕྱག་མེད།

If the mother's son has the necessary qualifications,
the *Gaden* throne is not sealed off to him.

The Gaden *throne is the highest seat of the Tibetan Gelugpa tradition of Tibetan Buddhsim—but it's not a hereditary position, so with the right qualities, anyone of any parentage can in principle occupy it. Akin to an exhortation to "Aim high, and shoot for the moon" or the encouragement that "Where there's a will, there's a way."*

About the Author

PEMA TSEWANG, SHASTRI, a former Fulbright scholar at Harvard University, has served as the chairman of the board of directors for the Tibetan Association of Boston, and has served in various capacities—as principal, headmaster, and teacher of Tibetan language, literature, and history—at schools in the Tibetan Children's Village, and as principal and administrator at the Institute for Buddhist Dialectics Dolmaling, both in Dharamsala, India. He currently works at Wisdom Publications, and has also published many books in Tibetan, including poetry, fiction and nonfiction, and translations of works by Dr. Gene Sharp and Charles Dickens. He lives in Somerville, Massachusetts, with his family.

About Wisdom Publications

WISDOM PUBLICATIONS is dedicated to offering works relating to and inspired by Buddhist traditions. To learn more about us or to explore our other books, please visit our website at www.wisdompubs.org. You can subscribe to our e-newsletter or request our print catalog online, or by writing to:

Wisdom Publications
199 Elm Street
Somerville, Massachusetts 02144 USA
617-776-7416
info@wisdompubs.org

Wisdom is a nonprofit, charitable 501(c)(3) organization and donations in support of our mission are tax deductible.

Wisdom Publications is affiliated with the Foundation for the Preservation of the Mahayana Tradition (FPMT).